Team Building

B. Vincent

Published by RWG Publishing, 2021.

TEAM BUILDING

First edition. July 9, 2021.

Written by B. Vincent.

Also by B. Vincent

Affiliate Marketing
Affiliate Marketing
Affiliate Marketing

Standalone
Affiliate Recruiting
Business Layoffs & Firings
Business and Entrepreneur Guide
Business Remote Workforce
Career Transition
Project Management
Precision Targeting
Professional Development
Strategic Planning
Content Marketing
Imminent List Building
Getting Past GateKeepers
Banner Ads
Bookkeeping

Bridge Pages
Business Acquisition
Business Bogging
Marketing Automation
Better Meetings
Conversion Optimization
Creative Solutions
Employee Recruitment
Startup Capital
Employee Mentoring
Servant Leadership
Team Building

Team Building

Casey Stengel once said, getting great players is simple, getting them to have together is the hard impact. Also, Henry Ford discloses to us meeting up as a start, remaining together as progress, and cooperating is achievement. Plainly recruiting great individuals in your organization is only the initial move towards hierarchical achievement. The genuine key is getting them to cooperate better. You need a group whose individuals know one another, see one another, trust one another, and can cooperate in a firm and viable way. How would we influence this sort of advancement in our colleagues, how would we frame the bonds and connections important to develop a perfectly tuned symphony our association needs? In this course, we'll tell you the best way to do precisely that.

Cooperation and coordinated effort are appraised as vital by 75% of bosses.

86% of representatives and chiefs said that absence of group building is the justification working environment disappointments. 97% of representatives emphatically concur that this association among laborers extraordinarily impacts the result of an undertaking or task. These measurements show that group building is an inexorably significant region that organizations should zero in on.

Our course will comprise of a progression of basic conversation focuses. These are intended to cover this wide point as altogether as could be expected, to empower development in these fundamental regions, and to work with a genuine and productive conversation, inside your association about how you can each enhance this fundamental trademark, both at work and in your own lives, as a rule.

A portion of these will be quite extensive and some will be somewhat direct and brief. At the finish of this guide, comes the main last advance. Conversation time, don't avoid this. This is the main piece of this preparation.

At the point when you finish this course, you need to go through somewhere around an hour or somewhere in the vicinity, going over the inquiries we supply toward the end, collectively. Whoever's the big boss with the gathering should assign a facilitator, whose obligation it is, that each question is covered and that everybody, time allowing, can express their opinion. Ensure all commitments are esteemed, all ideas considered and all feelings regarded.

So we should move into the principal conversation point.

Go out for lunch. This is presumably the most clear choice for any association, taking your group out for lunch is a standard for bosses to make connections between workers. Be that as it may, to zest things up, you can take out your group to a more uncommon spot. Presumably somewhere where they haven't all attempted previously. Whenever done right, bunch snacks will start the most healthy discussions, and assist with building more grounded connections. You can have these group snacks once per month, or after each euphoric event, like an effective lunch.

Simply make sure to change places around each time, to make it really intriguing.

Shock them with treats. You can unite your group all the more frequently by astonishing them with treats from time to time, getting a treat in the workday, when they least expected can fill their heart with joy. For instance, in the event that you two or three colleagues with a sweet tooth, pastries like frozen yogurt will get the job done. At lunch, you can draw out a frozen yogurt truck with an assortment of garnishes and flavors. You can likewise acquire solid and nutritious snacks for them to browse.

These basic yet unconstrained minutes permit your representatives to take a break, unwind and blend with other associates. Doing these sorts of things is likewise a way for you to say, thank you for your diligent effort. This will most likely lift them when they continue their work, for the remainder of the day.

Lease a house, an extraordinary end of the week escape is by leasing a sea shore house, or in the mountains. Pick an area that everyone will appreciate. You can investigate Airbnb and VRBO for such postings, having where you can discover natural air and enough daylight is useful for your wellbeing. Having a comfortable spot additionally allows your group to unwind and recalibrate when you get back from work. While there, you can amplify the time by making your group conceptualize novel thoughts. Truth be told, it doesn't need to be a conventional one, the solitary object is to consider how everybody can make a superior effect in your association.

Start a practice. There's something else entirely to celebrate than simply customary office festivities. At whatever point your group accomplishes something for the business, feel free to celebrate, even in the little successes.

Attempt to have a good time office party after your group achieves an achievement or completes large activities. Set out open doors to have some good times with your representatives a couple of times each year.

Make organization customs that each representative can celebrate. Here are some pleasant organization occasions that you can praise each year: food truck feast, run an occasion 5k, multicultural occasion random data night, carry your canine to work day, public pizza day. These office customs make each year energizing for your representatives, paying little heed to their way of life, race, or convictions. Having a festival after culture advances connection, supports work environment spirit, and builds efficiency.

Forager chase. What's group working without a round of forager chase? Scrounger chase is an exemplary outside game that urges individuals to work with different associates from various groups and divisions, developing cooperation and shaping new groups of friends in your organization. How does the game function? To start with, break the gathering into two groups or more. Make a rundown of things for them to discover or a rundown of entertaining errands that they ought to do, alongside a cutoff time to finish everything. Errands can incorporate taking a selfie with something sparkling, record your colleague lip-synchronizing, I like it as such, discovering somebody from another country, and record a video of them communicating in their language, and so forth Photographs and recordings ought to be partaken progressively on the gathering visit, as Facebook and slack. The principal group to do every one of the jobs is the champ. Forager chases are incredible for animating innovativeness, empowering authority, creating fellowship, boosting confidence, and venturing outside of your usual range of familiarity.

The minefield, the minefield is a great group building action intended to foster trust, correspondence, and undivided attention. How would you play this? To start with, you need to have an open space, for example, a meeting room, a vacant parking garage, a recreation center, or even at the sea shore, across the open space, dissipate irregular articles like balls, bottles, cones, plastic utensils, or anything protected and little enough to step on. These fill in as the personalities. Next have the gathering parted into sets, having one individual each pair blindfolded while the other one fills in as the guide, it is ideal to accomplice people with somebody that they don't know well, cooperation and trust will be scrutinized as accomplices will cooperate to break through to the opposite side, while staying away from the dispersed items.

The blindfolded accomplice will be the person who will cross the way, while the other one directs headings to get across to the opposite side. Be that as it may, there's a trick: the blindfolded one should not talk, the pilot is additionally not permitted to contact their accomplice. All things considered, the blindfolded, one should listen cautiously to their accomplice to stay away from the articles as they stroll across the opposite side. On the off chance that somebody hits a thing, they need to begin once more. After fix effectively arrives at the opposite side, they should switch positions and rehash the interaction. After the action, let the group answer these inquiries. For the individual blindfolded, how can it feel to just utilize your ears while strolling? For the individual directing, what was the test to get your accomplice to the opposite side?

How could it feel to begin once again in the wake of stepping on an article?

What does this action show us trust and correspondence in the working environment?

Round of conceivable outcomes.

A few exercises are speedy, yet enjoyable to do in each group building occasion. Round of potential outcomes is one of them. Split your group into gatherings, then, at that point give an item for each gathering, consistently, an individual needs to go up before the gathering and exhibit an interesting unusual use for that article. The remainder of the gathering will think about what the person in question is depicting. Give one moment to each gathering to conceptualize how to utilize the article, from various perspectives as could really be expected. Note that the individual in front isn't permitted to talk. The person who surmises the most for each gathering is the victor. The basic yet fun game moves innovativeness and advancement that can persuade the group to break new ground, for novel thoughts.

Two certainties and one untruth, two realities and one falsehood is a straightforward icebreaker game, particularly for new groups. In the first place, everybody needs to sit in a circle confronting one another, have every individual review two realities about themselves, alongside one falsehood. The falsehood ought to be reasonable, not overstated. Pick somebody to go first. Allow them to express their two realities and the lie in an irregular request without uncovering which will be which, then, at that point the others should figure which is the untruth, circumvent the circle until the turn is finished. This basic action can make ready for new compatibility and to assist with taking out snap decisions among partners. It additionally allows contemplative people in your group an opportunity to stand up and share something important to them.

Deal puzzle, exchange abilities are required for this great gay split everybody into little equivalent estimated gatherings. Give out a jigsaw puzzle with similar number of pieces for each gathering, the gathering who completes the riddle, the quickest successes. However, here's the curve, a few pieces are blended in with the other gathering's jigsaw puzzles. The genuine test is the means by which to get different pieces from the other gathering. This could be either through exchanging arranging, or in any event, trading bunch individuals, whatever their procedure is, everybody should choose as one. This action is an extraordinary method to improve your representatives relational abilities. Such abilities incorporate powerful correspondence, undivided attention, critical thinking, dynamic, self-assuredness, compatibility building.

The egg drop, an exemplary yet untidy approach to assemble affinity, the egg drop game. Make gatherings of three to five individuals and give each gathering a crude egg, give a container of various office supplies in 15 to 30 minutes, he should utilize the provisions to construct an improvised contraption that keeps the egg from getting broken when dropped. Office supplies can incorporate tape, pencils, cups, straws, papers, elastic groups, and so on When time's up, each gathering will drop their thingamabob from the subsequent floor, and see which egg endures the fall. This regular group building game is exceptionally captivating, permitting colleagues to bond and scrutinize their innovative abilities. Ensure you have an additional stock of eggs, and a ton of paper towels, as this will be 100% Messy.

Spot grants, a basic yet extraordinary approach to perceive workers' uncommon commitments, is by giving out spot grants. Each time you see a worker achieve a particular undertaking or assignment, give them blessing coupons on the spot. These can be anything from markdown sites like LivingSocial, Groupon, restaurant.com, or stockroom limits like Costco. You can likewise give out passes to neighborhood sports, expressions, or music occasions. It can likewise be a monetary reward or reward remuneration, giving out spot grants assembles a culture of featuring a worker's outstanding presentation, in the normal everyday exercises and tasks. It can likewise be utilized to perceive commitments that in any case may go undetected, for example, electing to work longer hours during a bustling week or filling in for a missing worker. Routinely distributing spot grants, gives acknowledgment as well as advances efficiency, rousing everybody to consistently perform on a significant level.

Go to meetings, classes, workshops. For your representatives to cooperate successfully collectively. They likewise need to turn out to be better as people. Going to meetings, courses and workshops can assist your representatives with growing an expert. Supporting your workers in going to these occasions expands their perspective in their present job, or field. Make associations and trade thoughts with an expert local area. Gain information and understanding from recent developments, most recent innovation patterns, and so forth Construct trust, dedication, and notoriety. Keep in mind, you support these sorts of exercises, not on the grounds that you're anticipating something consequently. Maybe, you do this to show that you care about their expert turn of events and that their upgrades, separately, will immensely affect their exhibition all things considered.

Chipping in, group building, isn't generally about playing the most interesting of games and goofiest of exercises, you additionally need your representatives to figure out how to reward the local area. Chipping in is an extraordinary group building action, not exclusively to assemble affinity yet in addition to help your group discover authentic importance, in the work they do.

Regardless of whether you're anticipating your first group chipping in experience or searching for better approaches to reward your local area. Here are a few thoughts that can help your group have an effect. Sort out a public cleanup, have a work environment pledge drive, support an adolescent games group, grow a local area garden, help the destitute, share your ability locally, amass care bundles. Why is chipping in such an engaging group building movement? Think about these reasons: it advances harmony, upgrades critical thinking abilities, diminishes pressure, mechanism for acquiring new abilities, makes corporate social duty, and assembles durable recollections.

Games. Get the pack out together after work and go to a nearby brandishing game, anyway genius games can be somewhat expensive. Provided that this is true, you can take off to less expensive ones like partner or semi-ace games. Games, be that as it may, are not just for unwinding and happiness. These occasions can likewise significantly affect your own gathering. Seeing the commitment and energy of beginners can be exceptionally irresistible for your own group, who knows, those small time players can fill in as motivation for your laborers to turn out to be more dedicated to their work.

Getaway room. Departure rooms are rapidly turning into a go-to movement for organization group structures. Essentially, you're secured a room loaded up with riddles and conundrums. Your representatives will cooperate on a period cutoff to discover hints and settle conundrums, and to get away from the room.

This is an incredible movement for testing out your group's rationale, persistence, and coordinated effort. You can divide your representatives into a few gatherings, and prize the group with the quickest getaway time.

Go-kart Racing. Nothing gets you amped up more than go-kart dashing. It's a great energy filled movement in an amicable contest that your group can appreciate. You can even build up a yearly go-kart truck rivalry and hand out a prize to the Fastest Employee of the Year. In the event that others are not in the state of mind to join, most go-kart offices have other diversion like computer games and a bar that they can use to take a break.

Arcade games. Let's be honest, you're never actually too old to even consider playing arcade games. These sentimentality filled games are incredible for unwinding and mitigating pressure. In the event that your region has an arcade close by, you can go with your group in the early evening and play till you drop. You can make the action considerably more fun, by parting them into groups and see who can get the most tickets. The triumphant group can be granted a gathering lunch or gift vouchers.

Cooking challenges. This action draws out the internal expert cook and your workers. Split the gathering into little groups and challenge them to cook something stunning. It very well may be an investigation, food with a particular fixing, or something local to a specific area or country. Discover a few appointed authorities to taste their food. After the triumphant gathering has been granted all can eat their manifestations together, a movement that draws out inventiveness while filling Stomachs, unquestionably a mutual benefit without a doubt.

Following, the hustle, and clamor of city life can be distressing, heading out to and from work five days per week. Why not enjoy a reprieve from the Metropolitan world and move to the mountains, to get some daylight and outside air. Climbing is an extraordinary method to loosen up those fixed muscles, sitting on an office seat for very nearly eight hours every day. Given that following is useful for our actual wellbeing, it likewise adds to better psychological wellness. Allowing your representatives an opportunity to loosen up and chill out, can be a major assistance to forestall burnout and decrease pressure.

Setting up camp. Setting up camp is the main alternative for end of the week escapes. Setting up camp is an extraordinary method to put a hold on from the metropolitan region, and immediately separate yourself from innovation. All things considered, when you're presented to the entirety of the cutting edge stuff each day. It's wonderful to carry on with a basic way of life sometimes. At dinnertime, you can collect around a huge fire, while toasting marshmallows and singing melodies, open air fire stories produce the most goosebumps, and make the most intense of chuckles that you'll at any point hear, give some assistance by setting up shelters, and preparing suppers together. When the experience is finished, your workers will have a more grounded friendship and the fondest of recollections. They'll get back to cooperate with more enthusiasm, dedication, and congruity.

Fishing. Fishing is a fun and compensating movement that you and your group should attempt. Fishing not just gives you the nutrient D you need, yet it's anything but a profoundly fulfilling experience, track down a neighborhood lake or lake, and bring your casting poles, split them into little gatherings and let each gathering position on various sides of the lake. Fishing sets aside time and this time permits individuals to turn out to be all the more close, as you trust that your casting pole will be pulled. You can talk and giggle about anything while at the same time taking a gander at the reasonable blue sky. It additionally assists them with chipping away at a shared objective, having a similar assurance in getting a fish, high fiving and clench hand knocking are ensured whenever you've gotten your first fish. Building a genuine association with your collaborators is a truly fulfilling thing that in any case will not occur in a corporate setting.

What's more, presently it's conversation time, the main piece of this preparation, whoever's the big enchilada in the gathering should assign a facilitator, whose duty it is, that every one of the inquiries you see on your screen is covered and that everybody, time allowing, can give their opinion. Ensure all commitments are esteemed, every one of the ideas considered and all conclusions regarded.

Don't miss out!

Visit the website below and you can sign up to receive emails whenever B. Vincent publishes a new book. There's no charge and no obligation.

https://books2read.com/r/B-A-QWUO-UDHQB

BOOKS 2 READ

Connecting independent readers to independent writers.

Also by B. Vincent

Affiliate Marketing
Affiliate Marketing
Affiliate Marketing

Standalone
Affiliate Recruiting
Business Layoffs & Firings
Business and Entrepreneur Guide
Business Remote Workforce
Career Transition
Project Management
Precision Targeting
Professional Development
Strategic Planning
Content Marketing
Imminent List Building
Getting Past GateKeepers
Banner Ads
Bookkeeping

Bridge Pages
Business Acquisition
Business Bogging
Marketing Automation
Better Meetings
Conversion Optimization
Creative Solutions
Employee Recruitment
Startup Capital
Employee Mentoring
Servant Leadership
Team Building

About the Publisher

Accepting manuscripts in the most categories. We love to help people get their words available to the world.

Revival Waves of Glory focus is to provide more options to be published. We do traditional paperbacks, hardcovers, audio books and ebooks all over the world. A traditional royalty-based publisher that offers self-publishing options, Revival Waves provides a very author friendly and transparent publishing process, with President Bill Vincent involved in the full process of your book. Send us your manuscript and we will contact you as soon as possible.

Contact: Bill Vincent at rwgpublishing@yahoo.com www.rwgpublishing.com

www.ingramcontent.com/pod-product-compliance
Lightning Source LLC
Chambersburg PA
CBHW032136050726

47590CB00008B/3125